NEW LEARNER OPTIMIZED

MW00613696

LEARN

hola!

SPANISH

IN 30 DAYS

MASTER COMMON SPANISH PHRASES, WORDS, & GREETINGS FOR FAST & SIMPLE COMMUNICATION & MEMORY RETENTION FOR NEW LEARNERS

INCLUDES:
Common Phrases & Words For Quick Communication

ADRIANA MUÑOZ

TABLE OF CONTENTS

TABLE OF CONTENTS

TABLE OF CONTENTS

TABLE OF CONTENTS

DAY 1

The first step to learn a new language is being familiar with its greetings and most basic phrases. Listed below are everyday expressions in spanish, with pronunciation guides, to help you enunciate them properly.

Fun fact: The inverted question mark (¿) is used in Spanish to previously inform the reader that a question will follow. The same goes for exclamations (¡). So if you see these signs, you already know what it is.

INFORMAL GREETINGS

- **¡Hola!** - Hi!
- **¿Cómo estás?** - How are you?
- **¿Qué pasa?** - What's up?
- **¿Qué tal?** - What's up?
- **¿Cómo te va?** - How are you?

HOW TO ANSWER

- **Bien, gracias** – Good, thank you
- **Bien, ¿Y tu?** - Good, and you?
- **Estoy bien, ¿Y tu?** - I'm good, and you?
- **Bien, ¿Y a 0?** - Good, what about you? (The response "Bien, ¿y a 5?" should only be used as an answer to "¿Cómo te va?")
- **Muy bien** – Very good
- **Estupendo** – Amazing
- **Regular** – So so
- **Mal** – Not ok
- **Fatal** - Really bad

FORMAL GREETINGS

Formal language is used in situations such as talking to a person with whom there is no in5macy, talking to a client, talking to a government authority or someone with an honorary 5tle (doctor, master, professor), for example.

"Tu" and "Usted" are two spanish ways of saying "you". The main difference is in the degree of formality of each one: "Tu" is for informal situations."Usted" is for formal situations.

> **Bien ¿y tu?** - Good, and you?
> The example sentence above can be interpreted as an informal sentence, because of the use of "tu".
>
> **Bien ¿y usted?** - Good, and you?
> The sentence above can be interpreted as formal, as "usted" was used.

Example dialog – TU
John: Buenos días, Paul, ¿Cómo estás? - Good morning
Paul, how are you? Paul: Estoy bien ¿Y usted? - I'm fine and you?
John Estoy bien, gracias. - I'm fine, thank you.

Example dialog – USTED
John: Buenas tardes, vuestra excelencia. - Good afternoon, your honor.
Paul: Buenas tardes, señor abogado. ¿Cómo estás usted? - Good afternoon, sir. How are you
John: Bien, ¿y usted? - Good, and you?
Paul: Nada demás, solo estoy de pasaje. Gracias. - No big deal, I'm just passing through, thank you.

HOW TO SAY "GOODBYE" (BOTH FORMAL AND INFORMAL)

- **Hasta luego** - See you later
- **Hasta pronto** - See you soon.
- **Hasta la vista** - See you soon.
- **Adiós** - Goodbye.
- **Chao** - Bye
- **Nos vemos** - We'll see.
- **Hasta mañana** - See you tomorrow.
- **Hasta la próxima semana** - Until next week.

As Spanish is a foreign language for you, you are not expected to understand everything the first time. You can get people's empathy and understanding by telling them a little about you.

For example:

- **Estoy aprendiendo español y todavía es diecil para mí entender.** - *I'm learning Spanish and it's still difficult for me to understand.*

- **Soy estudiante de español así que necesito que hables despacio, por favor.** - *I'm a Spanish student so I need you to speak slowly, please.*

DAY 2

FOR YOU TO KNOW A LITTLE MORE ABOUT SPANISH..

Spanish, also denominated Castilian, is the official language of Spain, in Europe; Argentina, Bolivia, Colombia, Costa Rica, Cuba, Chile, Ecuador, Guatemala, Honduras, Mexico, Nicaragua, Panama, Paraguay, Peru, Puerto Rico, Dominican Republic, El Salvador, Uruguay and Venezuela, in Latin America; and Equatorial Guinea, in Africa.

The Spanish language has variants that occur both within Spanish territory and in other countries that adopt it as an official language. These variants mainly concern pronunciation, vocabulary, intonation and the use of some pronominal forms. Due to its growing presence in the demographics and popular culture of the United States, especially in the fast-growing Sun Belt states, Spanish is the second most learned language by native English speakers. the growing

The political and economic stability of many of the largest Spanish-speaking nations, the immense geographic spread of the language in Latin America and Europe for tourism, and the growing popularity of culturally vibrant destinations found in the Hispanic world have contributed significantly to the growth of learning Spanish as a foreign language, all around the world. Currently, Spanish is the third most used language on the internet after English and Mandarin. It is also the second most studied language and the second language of international communication, after English, all over the world.

Some fun facts about Spanish are, for example:
- Spanish uses inverted exclamation and question marks;
- Like most languages, Spanish has its own very unique words which can't be translated into other languages;
- Spanish is the second most studied language in the world;
- Spanish has Latin origins.

DAY 3

ALPHABET AND PRONOUNCIATION

The Spanish alphabet has 29 symbols (27 **letters** and two digraphs: "LL" and "CH").The names of the **letters** of the Spanish alphabet are feminine (la a, la be, la ce, etc).

A a	B b	C c	D d	E e	F f	G g	H h	I i
a	be	ce	de	e	efe	ge	hache	i
[a]	[be]	[θe]	[de]	[e]	[efe]	[xe]	[atʃe]	[i]

J j	K k	L l	M m	N n	Ñ ñ	O o	P p	Q q
jota	ka	ele	eme	ene	eñe	o	pe	cu
[xota]	[ka]	[ele]	[eme]	[ene]	[eɲe]	[o]	[pe]	[ku]

R r	S s	T t	U u	V v	W w	X x	Y y	Z z
ere	ese	te	u	ve	doble ve	equis	i griega	zeta
[ere]	[ese]	[te]	[u]	[be]	[doble βe]	[ekis]	[i griega]	[θeta]

ARTICLES

The Spanish language distinguishes two genders, the masculine and the feminine. In this way we have the definite or determinate articles, and the indefinite or indeterminate ones.

	Singular	Plural	Singular	Plural
Masculino	EL	LOS	UN	UNOS
Feminino	LA	LAS	UNA	UNAS
Neutro	LO			

Articles announce the gender and number of a word.

Ex: El estudiante - masculine gender, singular number.

Do not confuse "el" article with "él" pronoun. The neuter article has no plural. Do not confuse "el" and "lo".

- Definite article: refers to known objects, precisely.
- Indefinite article: marks a noun in a vague way.
- Neutral article LO: does not refer to gender, number, or specific beings. It transforms an adjective with masculine determination into an abstract noun, typical of the Spanish language. Ex: lo bueno, lo false.

Other neutral article Functions:
- Before adverbs. Ex: Lo malo es que no tenemos comida.
- Before singular masculine possessive pronouns. Ex: Me gusta lo mío.
- Before: que, cual y más. Ex: Lo que te he dicho es la verdad / Lo más triste.

The articles are not used in front of the names of people, countries, cities that do not have a complement. Ex: Hoy hable com Pablo.

With the exception of:
- Names with complement: Yo soy la Maria de España and no la de Portugal;
- Family names: Los Garcías;
- Names of rivers, lakes, seas: El rio Amazonas;
- Countries like El Salvador;
- To talk about works by artists, compare famous people, sportsmen: El Picasso.
- Faced with titles, positions, forms of treatment, when we talk to the person: - Hola, Señor Pablo / El Señor Pablo es un hombre muy inteligente.
- Talking about professions: Él estudia Arquitectura.
- In front of possessives and demonstratives: Mi casa es bonita.

DAY 4

INTRODUCE OURSELVES, AGE, WHERE DO WE LIVE, HOBBIES.

Simply follow these steps, and you'll be well on your way to making a connection with someone:

- To say hello or hi, merely say "**Hola**";
- To introduce yourself, simply say "**Me llamo**", followed by your name;
- For example, "**Hola, me llamoPablo** means "Hi, I'm Pablo";
- To ask someone's name in a formal way, say "**¿Cómo se llama usted?**". This means "What is your name?". In an informal sesng, or if speaking to a child, say "**¿Cómo te llamas?**";
- After the person responds, you may say,"**Mucho gusto**", that means "Pleased to meet you"

The most common way to introduce yourself in Spanish is to say "Mellamo" followed by your name. Alterna5ves include "Mi nombre es" or "Soy" followed by your name. "Hola" can be used for either "hi" or "hello".

When you want to know somebody's age in English, you ask ,"How old are you?". You expect the person to answer by saying "I'm... years old." In Spanish, you won't use a form of "ser" (to be) or "estar" (to be) to say age. Instead, you use "tener" (to have).

To ask a person's age in Spanish, you'll use the phrase Cuántos años (How many years) plus a form of the verb tener(to have).This translates exactly as "How many years do/does ... have?", but the closest meaning in English is "How old are you?".

Here are some examples:

- *¿Cuál es tu/su edad? - What's your age?*
- *¿Cuántos años 5enes/5ene? - How old are you?*
- *¿Qué edad tienes? - How old are you?*
- *¿Cuántos años tiene tu hermana? - How old is your sister?*
- *Tengo catorce años - I am 14 years old.*
- *Mi madre tiene cincuenta años - My mother is 50 years old.*

In Spanish, you shouldn't omit the word años unless it has been used previously and the context makes clear what it means.

- ¿De dónde eres? (Where are you from? - informal)
- ¿De dónde es? (Where are you from? - formal)

- ¿A qué te dedicas? (What is your profession? - informal)
- ¿A qué se dedica? (What is your profession? - formal)

- ¿Estás visitando? (Are you visi5ng? - informal)
- ¿Está visitando? (Are you visi5ng? - formal)

DAYS OF THE WEEK:	MONTHS:	SEASONS:
Lunes Martes Miércoles Jueves Viernes Sábado Domingo	Enero Febrero Marzo Abril Mayo Junio Julio Agosto Sep5embre Octubre Noviembre Diciembre	Primavera Verano Outoño Invierno

NUMBERS:

1 – uno
2 – dos
3 – tres
4 – cuatro
5 – cinco
6 – seis
7 – siete
8 – ocho
9 – nueve
10 – diez
11 – once
12 – doce
13 – trece
14 – catorce
15 – quince
16 – dieciséis
17 – diecisiete
18 – dieciocho
19 – diecinueve
20 – veinte
21 – veintiuno
22 – veintidós
23 – veintitrés
24 – veinticuatro
25 – veinticinco
26 – vein5séis
27 – diecisiete
28 – dieciocho
29 – vein5nueve
30 – treinta
31 – treinta y uno

32 – treinta y dos
33 – treinta y tres
34 – treinta y cuatro
35 – treinta y cinco
36 – treinta y seis
37 – treinta y siete
38 – treinta y ocho
39 – treinta y nueve
40 – cuarenta
41 – cuarenta y uno
42 – cuarenta y dos
43 – cuarenta y tres
44 – cuarenta y cuatro
45 – cuarenta y cinco
50 – cincuenta
60 – sesenta
70 – setenta
80 – ochenta
90 – noventa
100 – cien
200 – doscientos
300 – trescientos
400 – cuatrocientos
500 – quinientos
600 – seiscientos
700 – setecientos
800 – ochocientos
900 – novecientos
101 – ciento uno
124 – ciento vein5cuatro
209 – doscientos nueve
212 – doscientos doce

302 – trescientos dos
347 – trescientos cuarenta y siete
410 – cuatrocientos diez
491 – cuatrocientos noventa y uno
514 – quinientos catorce
564 – quinientos sesenta y cuatro
603 – seiscientos tres
652 – seiscientos cincuenta y dos
729 setecientos vein5nueve
793 – setecientos noventa y tres
818 – ochocientos dieciocho
878 – ochocientos setenta y ocho
903 – novecientos tres
982 – novecientos ochenta y dos
1.000 – mil
2.000 – dos mil
3.000 – tres mil

ADJECTIVES:

Adjectives in Spanish are variable words that have the function of qualifying nouns, modifying them as they indicate their qualities and/or states.

Thus, adjectives appear before or after nouns, emphasize their characteristics and agree with them. Therefore, they undergo, in some cases, changes in gender (masculine and feminine), number (singular and plural) or degree (augmentative and diminutive).

In Spanish, there are two genders: feminine and masculine. To change a masculine adjective to the feminine gender, the "o" is usually replaced by "a", and vice-versa.

In general, adjec5ves also agree with nouns in number (singular and plural). To make this agreement, the leder -s is added.

Some examples of Adjectives:
- *Aburrido (bored)*
- *Alegre (happy)*
- *Sensible (sensi5ve)*
- *Fuerte (strong)*
- *Fácil (easy)*
- *Especial (special)*
- *Nuevo (new)*

DAY 5

PRONOUNS AND DETERMINERS

The determiners are words that usually precede the name and help to build its referential value. They give indications about what the name expresses, limiting or concretizing its meaning. They agree in gender and number with the noun. In turn, pronouns are words that replace a noun phrase. Unlike the determiner, pronouns cannot precede a noun.

This distinction also applies to possessives. Although the forms are the same, they are pronouns or determiners depending on their location and function in the sentence.

In other words:
A determiner occurs at the beginning of a noun phrase and in some way qualifies the rest of the noun phrase. A determiner cannot exist alone:

- **_Those_** classic songs were great.
- **_My_** car is the big one.

A pronoun can take the place of a whole noun phrase:
- **_Those_** were great classic songs.
- **_Those_** were great.
- **_Mine_** is the big one.

Personal pronouns replace a previously-men5oned noun. Use them to speak about yourself, or to address other people.
> _Example: Beatriz canta una canción. Ella canta una canción para ti._

Possessive pronouns indicate possession/belonging. We differentiate between dependent and independent possessive pronouns.
> _Example: Es mi maleta. (dependent) Es la mía. (independent)_

Relative pronouns introduce relative clauses.

    Example: La policía busca al hombre que atracó el banco.

Demonstrative pronouns include este, ese and aquel. We use demonstrative pronouns to point out something specific.

    Example: ¿Qué coche quiere comprar, este o aquel?

The reflexive pronouns are me, te, se, nos, os. We use them with reflexive verbs. Reflexive pronouns always refer to the subject.

    Example: Me miro en el espejo.

The **interrogative pronouns** are qué, quién and cuál. We use them to formulate questions.

    Example: ¿Quién ha dicho eso? ¿Qué ha dicho?

Some of the Spanish **indefinite pronouns** are algo, alguien, cualquiera, nada, ningún. We use them to generalise. There are two types of indefinite pronouns: dependent and independent.

    Example: No tengo ningún libro. (dependent) ¿Puedes prestarme alguno? (independent)

DAY 6

EXAMPLE DIALOGS

GREETINGS 1

Julia: ¿Qué tal, Carlos? ¿Cómo estás? **Carlos:** Bien gracias. ¿Cómo te va a ti? **Julia:** No muy bien. **Carlos:** ¿Qué pasa? **Julia:** Tengo dolor de cabeza. **Carlos:** Lo siento mucho; espero que te mejores pronto. **Julia:** Gracias. Nos vemos mañana.	**Julia:** What's up, Carlos? How are you? **Carlos:** Fine thank you. How about you? **Julia:** Not very well. **Carlos:** What's the mader? **Julia:** I have a headache. **Carlos:** I'm so sorry, I hope you get better soon. **Julia:** Thank you, see you tomorrow.

GREETINGS 2

Isabel: ¡Hola Enrique! **Enrique:** ¡Hola Isabel! ¿Como estas? **Isabel:** Bien, gracias. **Enrique:** ¿Como esta tu familia? **Isabel:** Todos bien. ¿Y tu familia? **Enrique:** Bien también. **Isabel:** ¿Que vas a hacer hoy, Enrique? **Enrique:** Nada. ¿Y tu? **Isabel:** Voy a estudiar un poco. **Enrique**: Bueno, me tengo que ir. Nos vemos. **Isabel:** Adios.	**Isabel:** Hi Enrique! **Enrique:** Hi Isabel! How are you? **Isabel:** Fine, thank you. **Enrique:** How is your family? **Isabel:** All good. And your family? **Enrique:** Good too. **Isabel:** What are you going to do today, Enrique? **Enrique:** Nothing. And you? **Isabel:** I'm going to study a lidle. **Enrique:** Well, I have to go. See you. **Isabel:** Bye.

LET'S GO SHOPPING!

- **Where can I buy … ?** - ¿Dónde puedo comprar … ?
- **Is there a store?** - ¿Hay aquí una 5enda?
- **Do you have … ?** - Tienen … ?
- **Show me, please.** - Muéstreme, por favor.
- **I need …** - Necesito de …
- **I like this one**. - Esto me gusta.
- **Can i try on?** - ¿Me lo puedo probar?
- **I need the size …** - Necesito la talla …
- **Do you have a bigger one?** - ¿Tiene(s) una talla más grande?
- **It looks good.** - Me queda(n) bien.
- **Where can I buy trousers?** - ¿Dónde puedo comprar pantalones?
- **I like this shirt.** - Me gusta esta camisa.
- **What's the price?** - ¿Cuánto cuesta(n)?
- **My size is 36.** - Soy talla 36.
- **I would like to buy this shirt, small size.** - Voy a llevar esta camiseta de la talla pequeña.
- **How can I get to the mall?** - ¿Cómo puedo llegar al centro comercial?
- **Where are the fiong rooms?** - ¿Dónde están los probadores?

HOW TO ORDER FOOD IN A RESTAURANT

- **I would like to reserve a table for … (number of people) at … (time).** - Me gustaría reservar una mesa para … a las …
- **A table for … (number of people), please.** - Una mesa para … , por favor.
- **Do you accept credit card?** - ¿Aceptan tarjetas de crédito?
- **Do you have vegetarian food?** - ¿Tienen comida vegetariana?
- **Do you have TV? We would like to watch the game.** - ¿Tienen televisiones? Nos gustaría ver el partido.

- **Can I see the menu?** - ¿Puedo ver el menú?
- **We would like to order, please.** - Nos gustaría ordenar por favor.
- **What do you recommend?** - ¿Qué nos puede recomendar?
- **Do you have any local typical food?** - ¿Tienen alguna especialidad local?
- **I am allergic to … . Does this dish contain … ?** - Soy alérgico/a a … . ¿Éste platillo contiene …?
- **We would like to eat …** , please - Me gustaría ordenar … , por favor.
- **I would like my meat rare/medium rare/well done** - Quisiera mi carne casi cruda/término medio/bien cocida.
- **One more, please!** - ¡Quisiera una más por favor!
- **We would like some desert.** - Nos gustaría ordenar un postre.
- **I don't drik alcohol.** - No tomo alcohol.
- **We would like to pay.** - Nos gustaría pagar la cuenta.
- **Keep the change.** - Quédese con el cambio.
- **My food is cold.** - Mi comida está fría.
- **I did not ask for this, I've asked for … .** - Yo no ordené esto, yo pedí … .
- **This is not clean.** - Ésto no está limpio.

FOOD

VEGETABLES	VEGETALES	FRUITS	FRUTA
asparagus	espárragos	apple	manzana
aubergine	berenjena	avocado	palta
beetroot	remolacha	banana	banana
brocolli	brócoli	cherry	cereza
cabbage	repollo	fig	higo
carrot	zanahoria	grape	uva
cauliflower	coliflor	grapefruit	pomelo
celery	apio	kiwi fruit	kiwi
cucumber	pepino	lemon	limón
eggplant	berenjena	lime	lima
fave beans	habas	orange	naranja
garlic	ajo	peach	durazno
lettuce	lechuga	pineapple	ananá
mushroom	hongo, champiñón	plum	ciruela
onion	cebolla	raspberry	frambuesa
peas	arveja	strawberry	frutilla
pepper	morrón	watermelon	sandía
potato	papa		
pumpkin	calabaza		
spinach	espinaca		
spring onion	cebolla de verdeo		
tomato	tomate		

MEAT	CARNE	FISH AND SEAFOOD	PESCADOS Y MARISCOS
bacon	tocino	anchovies	anchoas
beef	carne vacuna	cod	bacalao
chicken	pollo	hake	merluza
duck	pato	lobster	langosta
ham	jamón	mussels	mejillones
lamb	cordero	octopus	pulpo
pork	cerdo	prawns	langostinos
rabbit	conejo	salmon	salmón
ribbs	costillas	sardine	sardina
sirloin	lomo	shrimp	camarones
steak	bife	squid	calamar
turkey	pavo	trout	trucha
veal	ternera	tuna	atún
venison	venado		

ANIMALS

Are you a cat or a dog person? Regardless of what side you stand on, pets are often a good place to start a conversation about animals. Here are the names for some common pets in Spanish:

- El perro - **Dog**
- El gato - **Cat**
- El pez - **Fish**
- La tortuga - **Turtle**
- La serpiente – **Snake**
- El conejo - **Rabbit**
- El pollo - **Chicken**
- La vaca - **Cow**
- El toro - **Bull**
- La oveja - **Sheep**
- El caballo - **Horse**
- El cerdo/El puerco - **Pig**
- El burro - **Donkey**
- La cabra - **Goat**
- El ratón - **Mouse**
- El lobo - **Wolf**
- El oso - **Bear**
- La ardilla - **Squirrel**
- El cangrejo - **Crab**
- El delen - **Dolphin**
- La ballena - **Whale**
- El 5burón - **Shark**
- El pinguino - **Penguin**
- El elefante - **Elephant**
- El león - **Lion**
- La jirafa - **Giraffe**
- El mono - **Monkey**
- La mariposa - **Butterfly**
- La mosca - **Fly**
- La araña - **Spider**

Let's see some of these in context:

Voy a pasear el perro. - **I am going to walk the dog.**
Mi gato es blanco. - **My cat is white.**
Me gusta montar a caballo. - **I like to ride a horse.**
¡Cuidado, un 5burón! - **Look out, a shark!**
El león es el rey de la selva. - **Lions are the kings of the jungle.**
Las arañas me dan miedo. - **Spiders scare me.**

COLORS - LOS COLORES

- **Red** - Rojo
- **Blue** - Azul
- **Orange** - Anaranjado
- **Green** - Verde
- **Yellow** - Amarillo
- **Purple** - Morado
- **Pink** - Rosado

- **Black** - Negro
- **Brown** - Marrón
- **Violet** - Violeta
- **Lilac** - Lila
- **Gray** - Gris
- **Negro** - Preto
- **Blanco** - Branco

It's important to note that in Spanish, if you are referencing the word "orange", the translation would depend on whether you are talking about the color or the fruit. If you are talking about the color, you would use "anaranjado", whereas for the fruit, the word would be "naranja".

And what if I want to specify the tonality? Here are some examples:
- *Azul cian* - **Cyan blue**
- *Azul oscuro* - **Dark blue**
- *Olive green* - **Verde oliva**

ASK FOR DIRECTIONS

¿Cómo se va a... ?

Once you've got the local's adention, there are several ways you can ask them for direction:
- *Disculpa, ¿la catedral?*
- *Señor, ¿la entrada al museo?*
- *Buenas tardes. ¿La terminal de autobuses?*

You can also just tell them that you are looking for a certain place and it will be implied that you are expecting them to help you by giving you directions.
- Busco la estación del tren más cercana. - **I'm looking for the closest train station.**
- Estoy buscando un cajero automático. - **I'm looking for an ATM.**

You could also ask explicitly for directions in the following ways:
- ¿Dónde está el Museo de Arte Moderno? - **Where is the Museum of Modern Art?**
- ¿Dónde están las escaleras? - **Where are the stairs?**
- ¿Cómo llego al parque? - **How do I get to the park?**
- ¿Sabes si está por aquí el centro comercial? - **Do you know if the mall is around here?**
- ¿Hay un hospital cerca de aquí? - **Is there a hospital around here?**

Here are some other questions and phrases that might be useful when you are in a new place.

- Qué tan lejos está el/la... del/de la...? - **How far is the... from the...?**
- Dónde puedo tomar un taxi? - **Where can I take a taxi?**
- Pasa por aquí el camión que va a...? - **Does the bus to... pass by here?**
- Cuál es la mejor forma de ir a...? - **What is the best way to go to...?**
- Estoy perdido/a. - **I'm lost.**

- A la derecha - **Turn right**
- A la izquierda - **Turn left**
- Dirección única - **One way**
- Adelante - **Ahead**
- Atrás - **Behind**
- En frente - **In front**
- Lejos - **Far**
- Cerca - **Close**
- Al lado - **Next to**
- En - **At**
- Adentro - **Inside**
- Afuera - **Outside**
- Desde - **From**
- Hasta - **Until**

- Vaya - **Go**
- Camina - **Walk**
- Sigue - **Con0nue**
- Rodea - **Go around**
- Sube - **Go up**
- Baja - **Go down**
- Sale - **Go out**
- Entra - **Enter**
- Pasa por - **Pass by**

- La calle - **Street**
- La banqueta - **Sidewalk**
- La cuadra - **Block**
- La esquina - **Corner**
- La glorieta - **Roundabout**
- El camellón - **Median strip**
- El semáforo - **Traffic light**
- La entrada - **Entrance**
- La salida - **Exit**
- La taquilla - **Ticket office**

MODE OF TRANSPORTIONS

 Carro

 **Bicicleta**

 Patineta

 **Carruaje**

Motocicleta

 Taxi

 **Camioneta**

 **Bus**

 Camión

 Ambulancia

  **Metro (Subterrâneo)**

 **Tren**

 **Tractor**

 **Bote**

 Barco

 **Submarino**

Helicóptero

Avión

 Globo Aerostático

 Cohete

Adriana Muñoz

22

DAY 10

HOW TO ANSWER THE PHONE

- ¿Aló? - **Hello?**
- Oigo - **I hear**
- Diga - **Tell me**
- Buenos dias, habla Maria - **Good morning, Maria speaking**
- ¿Quién es? - **Who's calling?**
- Se ha equivocado - **You are mistaken (wrong number)**
- Perdón, no le en5endo - **Sorry, I don't understand**
- ¿Podría hablar com Maria? - **Can I speak with Maria?**
- ¿Puedo dejarle un recado? - **May I leave a message?**
- Favor de volver a llamar - **Please call back**
- No colgar - **Don't hang up**
- Esperar un momento - **Wait a moment**
- Deja su nombre y número - **Leave your name and number**
- Vuelve a llamar - **Call back**
- Te llamo luego - **I'll call you later**
- La línea está ocupada - **The line is busy**
- Lo siento, pero no me interesa - **Sorry, I'm not interested**
- Gracias por llamar - **Thank you for calling**
- Llámame más tarde - **Call me later**
- Tengo que colgarte - **I have to go**
- Me acaba la batería - **I'm almost out of battery**
- Tengo otra llamada - **I have another call**

WHAT TIME IS IT?

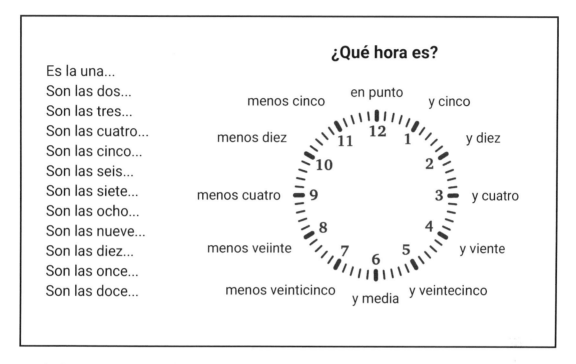

Es la una...
Son las dos...
Son las tres...
Son las cuatro...
Son las cinco...
Son las seis...
Son las siete...
Son las ocho...
Son las nueve...
Son las diez...
Son las once...
Son las doce...

¿Qué hora es?

menos cinco — en punto — y cinco
menos diez — y diez
menos cuatro — y cuatro
menos veiinte
menos veinticinco — y media — y veintecinco — y viente

To ask the 5me in Spanish, the most used expressions are:
- *¿Qué hora es?*
- *¿Qué hora 5ene?*
- *¿Tiene hora?*
- *¿Puede decirme qué hora es?*

To inform the time in Spanish, the verb "ser" (singular and plural) and the feminine articles la (a) and las (as) are used.

Examples:
- *Es la una Es mediodía*
- *Son las ocho*
- *Son las tres y media / Son las tres y treinta*

DAY 12

QUESTIONS

In Spanish, there may be several ways to ask the same question. The inverted question mark always begins a question.

The following questions mean exactly the same thing: Does Laura speak Spanish?
- *¿Laura habla español?*
- *¿Habla Laura español?*
- *¿Habla español Laura?*

Possible answers would be:
- *Sí, Laura habla español.*
- *No, Laura no habla español.*

Common words used to introduce other questions are:

- *¿Adónde?*
- *¿Dónde?*
- *¿De dónde?*
- *¿Cómo?*
- *¿Cuál?*
- *¿Cuándo?*
- *¿Cuánto?*
- *¿Qué?*

- *¿De qué?*
- *¿Quién?*
- *¿A quién?*
- *¿Con quién?*
- *¿De quién?*
- *¿Por qué?*
- *¿Para qué?*

Notice how the subject and verbs are inverted. That is, the subject comes after the verb:

- ¿Qué estudia Laura? - **What does Laura study?**
- ¿Dónde está mi coche? - **Where is my car?**

¿Dónde? means "Where?" ¿Adónde? means "To where?" In other words, "dónde" asks for a location, while "adónde" asks for a destination:

- ¿Dónde está Laura? - **Where is Laura?**
- ¿Adónde va Laura? - **Where is Laura going?**
- ¿De dónde? means **"From where?"**
- ¿Cómo? means **"How?"**
- ¿Cuál? and ¿Cuáles? mean **"What?" or "Which?"**
- ¿Cuándo? means **"When?"**
- ¿Cuánto? means **"How much?"**
- ¿Cuántos? means **"How many?"**
- ¿Qué? means **"What?"**
- ¿De qué? means **"About what?" or "Of what?"**
- ¿Quién? means **"Who?"**
- ¿A quién? means **"Whom?"**
- ¿Con quién? means **"With whom?"**
- ¿De quién? means **"Whose?"**
- ¿Por qué? means **"Why? (for what reason)"**
- ¿Para qué? means **"Why? (for what purpose)"**

DAY 13

 ¡ HABLEMOS ESPAÑOL !

ADVERBIALS OF PLACE

 ENCIMA (DE)
ON

 DEBAJO (DE)
UNDER

 **DENTRO (DE)**
OUT

 FUERA (DE)
IN

 DETRAS (DE)
BEHIND

 DELANTE (DE)
INFRONT OF

 A LA IZQUIERDA (DE)
ON THE LEFT

 A LA DERECHA (DE)
ON THE RIGHT

 AL FONDO (DE)
AT THE END

 ENFRENTE (DE)
OPPOSITE OF

 ENTRE... Y...
BETWEEN

 AL LADO (DE)
NEXT TO

- Ella vive cerca de la playa. - **She lives near the beach.**
- Los libros están encima de la mesa. - **The books are on the table.**
- Pusimos las cajas en el centro de la habitación. - **We put the boxes in the middle of the room.**

DAY 14

25 MOST USED SPANISH VERBS IN THE PRESENT TENSE

Ser To be	Estar To be	Hacer To do	Tener To have	Ir To go
• yo soy • tú eres • el es • nosotros samos • vosotros sois • ellos son	• yo estoy • tú estás • el esta • nosotros estamos • vosotros estáis • ellos están	• yo hago • tú haces • el hace • nosotros hacemos • vosotros haceis • ellos hacen	• yo tengo • tú tienes • el tiene • nosotros teriemos • vosotros tenéis • ellos tienen	• yo voy • tú vas • el va • nosotros vamos • vosotros vais • ellos van
Hablar To speak	**Coger** To get	**Vivir** To live	**Traer** To bring	**Beber** To drink
• yo hablo • tú hablas • el habla • nosotros hablamos • vosotros hablais • ellos hablan	• yo cojo • tú coges • el coge • nosotros cogemos • vosotros cogeis • ellos cogen	• yo vivo • tú vives • el vive • nosotros vivimos • vosotros vivis • ellos viven	• yo traigo • tú stem + traes • el stem + trae • nosotros stem + traemos • vosotros stem + traeis • ellos stem + traen	• yo bebo • tú bebes • el bebe • nosotros bebemos • vosotros bebeis • ellos beben

Necesitar To need	Tocar To touch	Querer To want	Deber To must	Poner To put
• yo necesito • tú necesitas • el necesita • nosotros necesita • vosotros necesitais • ellos necesitan	• yo toca • tú tocas • el toca • nosotros tocamos • vosotros tocais • ellos tocan	• yo quiero • tú quieres • el quiere • nosotros queremos • vosotros quereis • ellos quieren	• yo debo • tú debes • el debe • nosotros debemos • vosotros debeis • ellos deben	• yo pongo • tú pones • el pone • nosotros ponemos • vosotros poneis • ellos ponen
Poder To can	**Salir** To go out	**Buscar** To search	**Encontrar** To find	**Dormir** To sleep
• yo puedo • tú puedes • el puede • nosotros podemos • vosotros podeis • ellos pueden	• yo salgo • tú sales • el sale • nosotros salimos • vosotros salis • ellos salen	• yo busco • tú buscas • el busca • nosotros buscamos • vosotros buscáis • ellos buscan	• yo encumentro • tú encuentras • el encuentra • nosotros encontramos • vosotros encontráis • ellos encuentran	• yo duermo • tú duermes • el duerme • nosotros dormimos • vosotros dormis • ellos duermen

Saber To know	Dar To give	Trabajar To work	Comer To eat	Venir To come
• yo se • tú sabes • el sabe • nosotros sabemos • vosotros sabeis • ellos saben	• yo doy • tú das • el da • nosotros damos • vosotros dois • ellos dan	• yo trabajo • tú trabajas • el trabaja • nosotros trabajamos • vosotros trabajais • ellos trabajan	• yo como • tú comes • el come • nosotros comemos • vosotros comeis • ellos comen	• yo vengo • tú vienes • el viene • nosotros venimos • vosotros venis • ellos vienen

EXAMPLE DIALOGS

¿A qué te dedicas?

Ana: Hola Pablo.	**Ana:** Hi Pablo.
Pablo: Hola ¿Qué tal?	**Pablo:** Hi, how are you?
Ana: Estoy bien. ¿Estás trabajando?	**Ana:** I'm fine. Are you working?
Pablo: Sí, estoy trabajando en una tienda de regalos.	**Pablo:** Yes, I'm currently working at a gift shop.
Ana: ¿Qué haces exactamente?	**Ana:** What do you do exactly?
Pablo: Soy auxiliar de contabilidad. ¿Y tú a qué te dedicas?	**Pablo:** I'm an accoun5ng assistant. And you, what do you work on?
Ana: Yo estoy trabajando en la empresa de mi padre, soy secretaria pero pienso que muy pronto voy a tener un puesto mejor.	**Ana:** I'm working at my father's company, I'm a secretary but I believe I'll have a better positon soon.
Pablo: ¡Qué bueno!	**Pablo:** Good!

Apresentar una amiga

Paloma: ¡Hola, Pablo!

Pablo: ¡Hola! ¿Cómo estás?

Paloma: ¡Bien, gracias! ¿Y tú?

Pablo: Muy bien.

Paloma: Me alegro. Pablo, te presento a una muy buena amiga. Ella es Ana.

Ana: ¡Hola! Soy Ana Mendez.

Pablo: Encantado de conocerte. Soy Pablo Gardel.

Paloma: ¿Adónde vas?

Pablo: Estoy yendo a la biblioteca. Necesito buscar unos ar culos de diario para un caso que tenemos.

Paloma: Como siempre, trabajando tanto. Nosotras estamos yendo al centro comercial. Necesito unos zapatos.

Pablo: Bueno entonces, que la pasen bien.

Paloma: Gracias. Saludos a tus padres.

Pablo: ¡Cómo no! ¡Cuídate! Ana, muy lindo en conocerte.

Paloma: Hi Pablo!

Pablo: Hi! How are you?

Paloma: Fine, thanks! And you?

Pablo: Very good.

Paloma: I'm glad. Paul, I present to you a very good friend, Ana.

Ana: Hi! I am Ana Mendez.

Pablo: Nice to meet you. I am Pablo Gardel.

Paloma: Where are you going?

Pablo: I'm going to the library. I need to look up some newspaper articles for a case we've got.

Paloma: As always, working so hard. We are going to the mall. I need some shoes.

Pablo: Well then, have a good time.

Paloma: Thank you. Greetings to your parents.

Pablo: Why not! Take care of yourself! Ana, pleased to meet you.

LET'S CHOOSE WHERE TO EAT!

David: ¿Qué te gusta comer? ¿Adónde quieres cenar?	**David:** What do you like to eat? Where do you want to eat dinner?
Sonia: A mí me gusta la comida italiana, peruana y tailandesa.	**Sonia:** I like Italian, Peruvian and Thai food.
David: Me parece buena idea. A mí me apetece comer mariscos.	**David:** Sounds like a good idea to me. I am craving seafood.
Sonia: Vamos a comer ceviche entonces en un restaurante peruano.	**Sonia:** Then let's go eat ceviche at a Peruvian restaurant.

DAY 16

CLOTHES - LAS ROPAS

- la bata - dressing gown / bathrobe
- el bikini - bikini
- la blusa - blouse
- la bufanda - scarf
- los calce5nes - socks
- el calzón / la braga - underwear (for women)
- el calzoncillo - underwear (for men) / boxers
- la camisa - shirt
- la camiseta - t-shirt
- la chaqueta - jacket
- el cinturón - belt
- la corbata - 0e
- la falda - skirt
- la gorra - cap
- los guantes - gloves
- el impermeable - raincoat
- los jeans / los (pantalones) vaqueros - jeans
- las medias - 0ghts
- el overol / el mono - overalls
- el pantalón / los pantalones - pants / trousers
- el pijama - pijamas
- el short / el pantalón corto - shorts
- el sostén / el sujetador - bra
- el sombrero - hat
- la sudadera - sweatshirt
- el suéter / el jersey - sweater / jersey
- el traje - suit

- el traje de baño / el bañador - swimming trunks / swimsuit
- el uniforme - uniform
- el ves5do - dress
- las botas - boots
- las chanclas - flip flops
- las pantuflas - slippers
- las sandalias - sandals
- las zapa5llas - sport shoes / trainers / running shoes
- los zapatos - shoes
- el bolsillo - pocket
- el botón / los botones - bu^on / bu^ons
- el cierra - zip / zipper
- el cordón (de zapato) - shoelace
- la manga - sleeve
- la ropa interior - underwear

TALLA – SIZE
- Grande - large
- Mediano - regular
- Pequeño - small

FAMILY - LA FAMILIA

- I love being a part of a big family. - Me encanta formar parte de una familia grande.
- We're having a family reunion in Canada next summer. - Vamos a tener una reunión
- familiar en Canadá el verano que viene.
- It runs in the family. - Es cosa de familia.
- They treat her as one of the family. - La tratan como si fuera de la familia.
- Ideal for a family with 2-3 children or 2 couples. - Ideal para una familia con 2-3 niños o 2 parejas.
- This ranch has been in my family for five genera5ons. - Este rancho ha estado en mi familia por cinco generaciones.
- This could be a great opportunity for your family, Pablo. - Esto podría ser una gran oportunidad para tu familia, Pablo.

To start a family - Empezar a tener hijos
Family business - Negocio familiar
Family man - Hombre de familia
Family tree - Árbol genealógico
How is your family? - ¿Cómo está tu familia?
How many people are in your family? - Cuántos son en tu familia?

- Padre - father
- Madre - mother
- Hijo - son
- Hija - daughter
- Esposo - husband
- Esposa - wife
- Padres - parents
- Hermano - brother
- Hermana - sister
- Abuelos - grandparents
- Abuelo - grandfather
- Abuela - grandmother
- Nietos - grandchildren
- Nieto - grandson

- Nieta - grand-daughter
- Tío - uncle
- Tía - aunt
- Primos - cousins
- Primo - cousin (male)
- Prima - cousin (female)
- Sobrino - nephew
- Sobrina - niece
- Suegro - father-in-law
- Suegra - mother-in-law
- Yerno - son-in-law
- Nuera - daughter-in-law
- Cuñado - brother-in-law
- Cuñada - sister-in-law
- Padrastro - stepfather
- Madrastra - stepmother
- Hijastro - stepson
- Hijastra - stepdaughter
- Hermanastro - stepbrother
- Hermanastra - stepsister
- Medio hermano - half-brother
- Medio hermana - half-sister

Mis padres viven en España. - **My parents live in Spain.**
Tengo parientes en Francia. - **I have relatives in France.**

PROFESSIONS /OCCUPATIONS

- medico - doctor
- ingeniero - engineer
- arquitecto - architect
- abogado - lawyer
- peluquero - hairdresser
- carpintero - carpenter
- farmacéu5co - pharmacologist
- bomber - fireman
- jardinero - gardener
- secretario - secretary
- mecánico - mechanic
- músico - musician
- enfermero - nurse
- fotógrafo - photographer
- psicólogo - psychologist
- cien fico - scien0st

- camarero - waiter
- professor - teacher
- bailarín - dancer
- administrador - administrator
- director - director
- agricultor - farmer
- pescador - fisher
- vendedor - sales person
- traductor - translator
- escritor - writer
- poeta - poet
- atleta - athlete
- florista - florist
- periodista - journalist
- recepcionista - recep0onist
- taxista - taxi driver

¿En qué trabajas? - **What do you do?**

¿A qué te dedicas? - **What do you do?**

¿Cómo es tu trabajo? - **What is your job like?**

¿Qué tal va tu trabajo? - **How is your job going?**

¿Te gusta tu trabajo? - **Do you like your job?**

¿Qué es lo que más te gusta de tu trabajo? - **What do you like the most about your job?**

¿Qué es lo que menos te gusta de tu trabajo? - **What do you like the least about your job?**

¿Cuál es tu horario de trabajo? - **What are your working hours?**

¿Qué te gustaría ser de mayor? - **What would you like to be when you grow up?**

Soy..., ¿y tú? - **I am a..., and you? (informal)**

Soy..., ¿y usted? - **I am a..., and you? (formal)**

Me dedico a... - **I work in...**

Trabajo en... - **I work in...**

Siempre quise ser... - **I have always wanted to be a...**

Me gusta mi trabajo. - **I like my job.**

Other example:

- *A: ¿A qué se dedica tu hermana? - **What is your sister's job?***
- *B: Trabaja como ingeniera. - **She works as an engineer.***

Here, you have an example of a person talking about their job:

Hola, me llamo Paloma. Soy medica. Trabajo en un hospital de lunes a viernes de 7 de la mañana a 3 de la tarde. Me gusta mucho mi trabajo. Desde que era niña siempre quise ser enfermera.

(Hi, my name is Paloma. I am a doctor I work in a hospital from Monday to Friday, from 7 a.m. to 3 p.m. Ever since I was a child, I wanted to be a doctor.)

DESCRIBING SOMEONE

¿Cómo eres? - What do you look like?

Soy... - I am...

¿Cómo es tu hermana? - How does your sister look like?

Es... - She / He is...

Tengo - I have

Tiene – She / He / It has

Tienes – You have

¿Cómo 5enes el pelo? - What is your hair like?

¿Cómo son tus ojos? - What are your eyes like?

Mi hermana 5ene los ojos marrones - My sister has brown eyes.

¿Llevas gafas? - Do you wear glasses?

Mi abuelo lleva barba y bigote - My grandfather has a beard and a moustache.

Tengo pecas - I have freckles.

ALTO-A / BAJO

DELGADO-A / GORDO-A

FEO-A / GUAPO-A

MAYOR / JOVEN

CALVO-A

CASTAÑO-A / MORENO-A

RUBIO-A / PELIRROJO-A

SER

Yo	**soy**
Tú	**eres**
Él / Ella Usted	**es**
Nosotros / Nosotras	**somos**
Vosotros / Vosotras	**sois**
Ellos / Ellas / Ustedes	**son**

¿Como eres?
How do you look like?
Soy alta y rubia
I'm tall and blonde
¿Cómo es él?
How does he look like?
Él es delgado y calvo
He is thin and bald

EL PELO

RIZADO / ONDULADO / LISO

CORTO / LARGO

RECOGIDO / SUELTO

MORENO / CASTAÑO / RUBIO / PELIRROJO / CANOSO / TEÑIDO

LOS OJOS

NEGROS   VERDES   MARRONES   AZULES   **UN LUNAR / PECAS**

LA NARIZ

GRANDE / PEQEUÑA

TENER

Yo	**tengo**
Tú	**tienes**
Él / Ella Usted	**tiene**
Nosotros / Nosotras	**tenemos**
Vosotros / Vosotras	**teneiés**
Ellos / Ellas / Ustedes	**tienen**

¿como tienes el pelo??

what is your hair like?

yo tengo el pelo rubio y largo

como tiene el pelo ella?

what is her hair like?

ella tiene el pelo corto y canoso

como tienes los ojos?

what are your eyes like?

Yo tengo los ojos marrones

como tiene los ojos el?

what are his eyes like?

él tiene los ojos azules

When it comes to colors, it's important to know the colors as they help to describe a person's hair:
- Blonde - rubio
- Brown - moreno
- Red - pelirrojo

Of course, a person's hair type will also set them apart from others:
- Curly - rizado
- Straight - lacio
- Wavy - ondulado
- Long hair - pelo largo
- Short hair - pelo corto

No hair? Él es calvo (He is bald) will get the point across!

OTHER IMPORTANT EXPRESSIONS

- **Yo no comprendo** - I don't understand
- **No me acuerdo** - I don't remember
- **Yo soy de...** - I came from...
- **¿En5ende?** - Do you understand?
- **¿Hablas inglés?** - Do you speak English?
- **¿Puede ayudarme?** - Can you help me?
- **No lo sé** - I don't know!
- **¡Lo siento!** = Sorry!
- **¿Qué significa ...?** - What does ... mean?
- **¿Puede repe5rlo?** - Can you say that again?
- **¿Dónde está el baño?** - Where is the bathroom?
- **¡Buen viaje!** - Have a good trip!
- **¡Cuídate! -** Take care!
- **¡Felicitaciones!** - Congratula0ons!
- **¡Salud!** - Cheers!
- **Mi favorito es...** - My favourite is...
- **¿Pasa algo?** - Is something wrong?
- **¿Sabes qué pasa?** - Do you know what's going on?
- **¿Me he equivocado?** - I was wrong?
- **¿Estás listo/a?** - Are you ready?
- **Que te mejores** - Get well soon
- **¿De verdad?** - Really
- **Llámame cuando llegues** - Call me when you arrive
- **¿Cuál es tu número de teléfono?** - What is your phone number?

- **¿Puedo entrar?** - Can I come in?
- **¡Feliz cumpleaños!** - Happy birthday!
- **¡Buena suerte!** - Good luck!
- **¿Hay alguien a quien pueda llamar en caso de fallo/avería?** - Is there anyone I can call in case of problem?
- **Te extraño** - I miss you
- **Te quiero** - I love you
- **¡Llame a una ambulancia! -** Call an ambulance!
- **¡Llame a la policía!** - Call the police!
- **¡Ten cuidado!** - Be careful!
- **Me han robado** - I've been robbed
- **Lo siento, pero tengo que irme** - Sorry, but I have to go
- **Estoy de acuerdo con usted** - I agree with you
- **No pasa nada** - No worries
- **¿Le puedo hacer una pregunta?** - May I ask a ques0on?
- **No he oído lo que ha dicho** - I couldn't hear what you said

PARTES DE LA CASA:

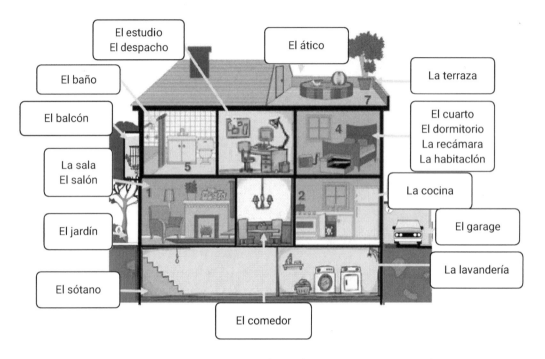

First, we should say if we live in a house (casa) or an apartment (departamento).

Some kitchen items are, for example:

- El horno - the oven
- La heladera - the fridge
- La cuchara - the spoon
- El tenedor - the fork
- El cuchillo - the knife
- El plato - the plate
- El vaso - the cup
- La taza - the mug
- La ba5dora - the blender

- La olla - the dutch oven
- La sartén - the pan
- El microondas - the microwave
- La pileta / la bacha - the sink
- La mesada - the kitchen counter
- La mesa - the table
- La silla - the chair
- El lavaplatos - the dishwasher

Some living room items are, for example:
- La mesita - the coffee table
- La ventana - the window
- Las cor5nas - the curtains
- El teléfono - the telephone
- La alfombra - the carpet
- El almohadón - the cushion
- El sillón - the couch
- La tele / el televisor - the TV
- La lámpara - the lamp
- La chimenea - the chimney
- El cuadro - the pain5ng
- El reloj - the clock

Some bathroom items are, for example:
- El indoor - the toilet
- La ducha - the shower
- La bañera - the tub
- El secador - the hair dryer
- La toalla - the towel
- La esponja - the sponge
- El jabón - the soap
- El cepillo de dientes - the toothbrush
- El papel higiénico - the toilet paper
- El espejo - the mirror

Some bedroom items are, for example:
- La cama - the bed
- La mesita de luz - the night table
- El placard - the closet
- El escritorio - the desk
- La percha - the hanger
- La cuna - the crib
- Las sábanas - the sheets
- Los juguetes - the toys

Other random things that we have around our houses are, for example:
- La escoba - the broom
- La aspiradora - the vacuum cleaner
- El enchufe - the plug
- La llave - the key
- La basura - the garbage
- La computadora - the computer
- Las escaleras - the stairs
- Las cajas - the boxes

Here are some adjectives that can help you describe your house:
- Luminoso/a - luminous
- Grande - big
- Pequeño/a - lidle, small
- Elegante - fancy
- Moderno - modern
- Desordenado/a - un5dy
- Ordenado/a - 5dy
- Cálido/a - warm
- Frío/a - cold
- Cómodo/a - comfortable
- Hogañero/a - homely

DAY 22

PLACES AND BUILDINGS

- Cash machine - Cajero automático
- Park - Parque
- Shoe shop - Zapatería
- Book store - Librería
- Bridge - Puente
- Gas station - Gasolinera
- Hospital – Hospital
- Bus stop - Parada de autobús
- Restaurant - Restaurante
- Square - Plaza
- Bycicle path - Ciclovía
- Youth hostel - Albergue juvenil
- Grocery store - Supermercado
- Pharmacy – Farmacia
- Airport - Aeropuerto
- Street – Calle
- Church - Iglesia
- Tourist information center - Centro de información turística
- Clothing store - Tienda de ropa
- School - Escuela
- Monument – Monumento
- Factory - Fábrica
- Parking lot – Estacionamiento
- House - Casa
- Palace – Palacio
- Library – Biblioteca
- Gym – Gimnasio
- Fire sta0on - Parque de bomberos

- Amusement park - Parque de diversiones
- Kindergarten - Escuela infantil
- Police station - Comisaría
- Nature reserve - Reserva natural
- Art gallery - Galería de arte
- Train station - Estación de tren
- Bakery - Panadería
- Swimming pool – Piscina
- Music store - Tienda de música
- Sports arena - Estadio depor5vo
- Museum – Museo
- Bank – Banco
- Travel agency - Agencia de viajes
- Barber shop - Barbería

DAY 23

ADVERBS

Los adverbios (the adverbs) are invariable words used to modify the meanings of verbs, adjectives or other adverbs.

Adverbs can indicate affirmation, intensity, doubt, place, mode, nega5on, order and time.

Trabajas mucho. - You work a lot.

> **Note** that in the sentence above, the adverb mucho modifies the verb trabajar (to work) by adding a sense of intensity to it.

The example sentence not only expresses that Pablo has work, but also that he has a lot of work.

Here's a short Spanish adverbs list, with examples of how each one is used:
- **Antes** (Before)
  Antes de comer aceitunas prefiero patatas fritas. - Before ea5ng olives, I'd prefer chips.
- **Ahora** (Now)
  Ahora voy al gimnasio. - I am going to the gym now.
- **Todavía** (Yet)
  Todavía no me han llegado los pedidos. - My orders haven't arrived yet.
- **Mucho** (A lot)
  Yo voy mucho al gimnasio. - I go to the gym a lot.

- **Normalmente** (Normally)

  Normalmente mi padre tiene pan en casa. - Normally, my dad has bread at home.
- **A veces** (Sometimes)

  A veces salgo a patinar por el paseo marí5mo. - Sometimes I go roller skating along the seaside.
- **Aquí** (Here)

  Aquí en España hay muchos extranjeros. - Here in Spain, there are many foreigners.
- **Cerca** (Near)

  La biblioteca está cerca de mi casa. - The library is near my place.
- **Mejor** (Beder)

  Jose canta mejor que Luisa. - Jose sings beder than Luisa.
- **Así** (This way)

  Es así como 5enes que hacer los ejercicios. - You should do the exercises this way.
- **Mucho** (Very much)

  Me gusta mucho el cine. - I like the cinema very much.
- **Nada** (At all)

  No me gusta nada la música clásica. - I don't like classical music at all.
- **Seguramente** (Probably)

  Seguramente fue Juan el que más corrió. - Juan was probably the one who ran the most.
- **Tampoco** (Either, Neither)

  Nosotros tampoco sabemos la fecha del vuelo. - We don't know the flight's date either.
- **Quizá** (Perhaps, Maybe)

  Quizá se equivocaron al hacer la cuenta. - Maybe they were wrong when they prepared the bill.
- **Por qué** (Why)

  ¿Por qué 5enes sueño? - Why are you sleepy?
- **Como** (As)

  Como tú mandes. - As you wish

DAY 24

HOBBIES AND FREE TIME

I like... - Me gusta...
Me interesa... - I am interested in...

Pasatiempo - Hobby
Tiempo libre - Free time

¿Qué haces en tu 5empo libre? - What do you do in your free time?

- **Sports** - Deportes
- **To run** - Correr
- **To swim** - Nadar
- **To dance** - Bailar
- **To play** - Jugar
- **Soccer** - Fútbol
- **Basketball** - Baloncesto

- **To camp** - Acampar
- **To fish** - Pescar
- **Gardening** - Jardinería
- **Music** - Música
- **To sing** - Cantar
- **To play** - Tocar

(You can use "tocar" to say that you play an instrument. For instance, "toco el clarinete" means "I play the clarinet." While in English "to play" can be used with games, sports or instruments, in Spanish there is a clear distinction between two words that can mean "to play": "jugar" and "tocar". "Jugar" is used to discuss playing games and sports. "Tocar", which is usually translated as "to touch," is used to mean "to play" an instrument.)

- **Instrument** - Instrumento
- **To listen** - Escuchar
- **Art** - Arte
- **Photography** - Fotograea
- **To draw** - Dibujar
- **To paint** - Pintar
- **To sew** - Coser

- **To cook** - Cocinar
- **To write** - Escribir
- **Theater** - Teatro
- **To read** - Leer
- **To play cards** - Jugar cartas
- **To go shopping** - Ir de compras

DAY 25

<u>AT THE HOTEL</u>

Where is the hotel ... ? - ¿Dónde está el hotel ... (la pensión ...)?
Can you recommend a good hotel? -¿Puede usted recomendarme un buen hotel?
Is there any near by? - ¿Hay por aquí?

<u>AT THE HOTEL RECEPTION:</u>
- **For one night (two days, one week, one month)** - Para una noche (dos dias, una semana, un mes)
- **I made a reserva0on**. - He reservado aqui uma habitación.
- **Is there a room for one / two available?** - ¿Tienen una habiatción individual / doble libre?
- **What's the price per night?** - ¿Cuanto cuesta la habitacion por noche?
- **It is possible to add one more bed for my baby / kid?** - ¿Podrian poner una cama adicional (una cama de niño, una cuna)?

<u>PERSONAL DATA YOU NEED TO KNOW / DOCUMENTS OF THE GUEST:</u>
- Rellenar (preencher) un impreso, formulario, planilla o forma - **Fill a form with your information**
- Presentar (apresentar) original / fotocopias de documentos - **Provide photocopies of requested documents**
- Documento Nacional de Iden5dad (cédula de iden5dad) - **Identity card**
- Pasaporte - **Passport**
- Carné de conducir (licencia de manejar)- **Driving license**
- Nombre, primer apellido, segundo apellido - **Name, surname, other names**
- Nacionalidad, lugar/fecha de nascimiento - **Nationality, place and date of birth**
- Edad/ Estado Civil - **Age and civil status**
- Profesión/ocupación - **Profession / occupation**
- Lugar de residencia habitual (localidad, provincia, distrito postal) / domicilio /dirección - **Residence**

OTHER EXPRESSIONS:

- **In a quiet place.** - En un local tranquilo.
- **Where is my luggage?** - ¿Donde está mi equipaje?
- **Do you have a parking spot?** - ¿Tienen garaje (aparcamiento; playa de estacionamiento, parqueaderol)?
- **Is there any discount for kids?** - ¿Hay una rebaja / descuento para niños?
- **What time does the bus leave to ... ?** - ¿Cuándo sale el autobúspara ... ?

HOTEL VOCABULARY

air the room	airear la habitación
ashtrays	ceniceros
bath	bañera
bath gel	gel de baño
bathroom cleaner	limpiador de baño
bathroom sink	lavabo
bed	cama
bin	papelera
bin bags	bolsas de basura
bin liners	bolsas de basura
biscuit	galleta
blanket	manta
brass	bronce
brown sugar	azúcar morena
brush	cepillos / cepillar
chandeliers	araña de luces
check	comprabar
clean	limpio - limpiar
cleaner	producto para la limpieza
cobwebs	telarañas
conference pads	cuadernos para conferancias
cream	nata,crema
crockery	loza
cupboard	alacena - ropero
curtains	cortinas
cushions	cojines
decaffeinated coffee	café descafeinado
delivery sheets	reparto de sábanas

HOTEL VOCABULARY

• **departure**	• salida
• **de-scale**	• quitar la cal
• **desk**	• monstrador
• **dirt**	• suciedad
• **dirty**	• sucio
• **door handles**	• pomos de las puertas
• **doorstop**	• tope de las puerta
• **drawers**	• cajones
• **dust**	• quitar el polvo
• **duties**	• obligaciones
• **empty**	• vaciar , vacío
• **ensure**	• asegurarse de
• **envelopes**	• sobres
• **fan**	• ventilador
• **fill**	• rellenar -llenar
• **floor**	• piso, suelo
• **fold**	• doblar
• **furniture**	• muebles, mobiliario
• **glass cleaner**	• limpiacristales
• **glass doors**	• puertas de cristal
• **glass shelves**	• estanterías de cristal
• **guests**	• huéspedes
• **leads**	• cables
• **ledges**	• repisas
• **lid**	• tapa
• **lights**	• luces
• **lime**	• cal
• **linen**	• ropa blanca - sábanas
• **lobby**	• vestíbulo

• **lost property**	• objeto perdido
• **make sure**	• asegurarse de
• **menu**	• menú
• **mirror**	• espejo
• **mop**	• fregar, limpiar
• **neatly**	• con esmero
• **pads**	• cuadernos
• **pictures**	• cuadros
• **pillow**	• almohada
• **pillowcases**	• fundas de almohada
• **plug**	• tapón, enchufe
• **plug hole**	• tubo de salida, salida/ orificio para el enchufe
• **plump**	• mullir
• **polish property**	• limpiar, encerar, sacar brillo correctamente
• **public areas**	• áreas públicas, zonas
• **pull away**	• quitar, rodar
• **pull tight**	• alisar, estirar
• **quilt**	• colcha, edredón
• **radiator**	• radiador
• **reception**	• recepción
• **remove**	• quitar
• **replace**	• reemplazar, campiar
• **replenish**	• rellenar
• **rinse out**	• limpair, enjuagar, aclarar
• **roller towel**	• porta toallas de papel
• **room service folder**	• carpeta/folleto del service de habitaciones

HOTEL VOCABULARY

• **rubbish**	• basura
• **run out**	• quedarse sin , terminarse
• **scrub**	• fregar, restregar
• **servicing**	• abastecer , proveer , servir
• **shampoo**	• champú
• **sheets**	• sábanas
• **shower head**	• alcachofa(de la ducha)
• **shower hose**	• manguera(de la ducha)
• **signs**	• señales, carteles, placas
• **sill**	• fregadero ,pila, lavabo
• **sink**	• rodapié
• **skirting board**	• mancha
• **smear**	• jabón
• **soap**	• Jabonera
• **soap dish**	

HOW AM I FEELING TODAY?

CALM
CALMADO/A

HAPPY
FELIZ

SAD
TRISTE

SILLY
GRACIOSO/A

NERVOUS
NERVIOSO/A

ANNOYED
FASTIDIADO/A

TIRED
CANSADO/A

SHY
APENANO/A

SURPRISED
SOPRENDIDO/A

HUNGRY
HAMBRIENTO/A

ANGRY
ENOJADO/A

CONFUSED
CONFUNDIDO/A

SLEEPY
SOÑOLIENTO/A

SICK
ENFORMO/A

HURT
LASTIMADO/A

EMBARRASED
AVERGONZADO/A

DISAPPOINTED
DECEPCIONADO/A

WORRIED
PREOCUPADO/A

EMOTIONAL
EMOCIONAL

ANXIOUS
ANSIOSO/A

- ¡Me siento de maravilla! - **I feel great!**
- Me siento relajada. - **I feel relaxed.**
- Me siento como una princesa. - **I feel like a princess.**

These two verbs are kind of interchangeable. For example, you can either use "estar" or "sentirse" and it will mean exactly the same thing like "I feel angry" vs "I am angry."

However, "Carol feels sick" and "Carol is sick" might be a lidle bit different: When you say "Carol feels sick", she might have a horrible bout of gastro but she might also have a headache as she hasn't had her coffee this morning. So when you use "to feel", it's more about how she feels rather than whether she actually has some affliction. However, when you say "Carol is sick", it sounds like a proven fact. It's more definite.

If you want to say you are feeling like something, just add "como".
- Paloma tiene ansiedad. - **Paloma is anxious.**

The most common uses of tener to express feelings or emo5ons in Spanish include:
- **tener miedo de** – to be afraid of
- **tener sueño** – to be sleepy
- **tener ansiedad** – to be anxious
- **tener celos** – to be jealous
- **tener verguenza** – to be embarrassed
- **tener calma** – to be calm
- **tener esperanza** – to have hope
- **tener nervios** – to be nervous

To ask **"How do you feel?"**, say "¿Cómo te sientes?"
To say **"a little"** or **"a tiny bit"**, use "un poco" or "un poquito". Use "muy" to say"very".

EXAMPLE DIALOGS

CALLING THE AIRLINE TO CHECK FLIGHT

Javier: Hola, ¿Hablo a líneas aéreas Taca?

Esmeralda: Sí, señor. ¿Dígame en que le puedo ayudar?

Javier: Llamo porque necesito confirmar mi vuelo a Noruega esta tarde, a las 5:30.

Esmeralda: ¿Cuál es su nombre?

Javier: Mi nombre es Javier Hernández.

Esmeralda: Perdón. ¿Me podría repe5r su apellido?

Javier: Es Hernández, se deletrea H-E-R-N-AN-D-E-Z.

Esmeralda: Un momento por favor.

Javier: Gracias.

Esmeralda: Hernández ... hmm... si el vuelo número NE 6245 a Noruega, saldrá a las 5:30 pm.

Javier: ¿Hay algún retraso?

Esmeralda: Hmm... no, este vuelo está programado a tiempo por el momento, pero tiene que estar aquí una hora antes de partir.

Javier: Está bien, gracias.

Esmeralda: De nada, estoy para servirle.

Javier: Hi, do I speak with Taca airlines?

Esmeralda: Yes Sir. Tell me how can I help you?

Javier: I'm calling because I need to confirm my flight to Norway this afternoon, at 5:30.

Esmeralda: What is your name?

Javier: My name is Javier Hernández.

Esmeralda: Excuse me, could you repeat your family name to me?

Javier: It is Hernández, it is spelled H-E-R-NA-N-D-E-Z.

Esmeralda: One moment please.

Javier: Thank you.

Esmeralda: Hernández ... hmm...yes, the flight number NE 6245 to Norway will leave at 5:30 pm.

Javier: Is there any delay?

Esmeralda: Hmm... no, this flight is scheduled on 5me for now, but you have to be here an hour before departure.

Javier: That is fine, thank you.

Esmeralda: You're welcome, I am here to serve you.

FREE TIME

Pablo: ¿Qué haces normalmente en tu 5empo libre?
Carlos: Por semana voy a la piscina. Me gusta mucho nadar.
Pablo: ¿Vas solo o con amigos?

Carlos: Prefiero ir solo. Pero a veces voy con un amigo.
Pablo: ¿Y qué te gusta hacer los fines de semana?
Carlos: Los sábados duermo toda la mañana. Por la tarde, bebo unas cervezas con amigos. Y no hago nada más.
Pablo: ¿Y qué haces los domingos?

Carlos: Depende. Prefiero estar en casa y no hacer nada. Pero algunos domingos, voy al cine.
Pablo: Increíble. ¡Qué vago eres!

Pablo: What do you normally do in your free time?
Carlos: Every week I go to the pool. I really like swimming.
Pablo: Are you going alone or with friends?

Carlos: I prefer to go alone. But sometimes I go with a friend.
Pablo: And what do you like to do on weekends?
Carlos: On Saturdays I sleep all morning. In the afternoon, I have a few beers with friends. And I don't do anything else.
Pablo: And what do you do on Sundays?
Carlos: It depends. I prefer to be at home and do nothing. But some Sundays, I go to the movies.
Pablo: Unbelievable. How lazy you are!

AT THE RESTAURANT

José: Hola, Elena. Bienvenida a mi cena española.

Elena: Gracias por invitarme. ¿Te ayudo con algo?

José: No hace falta. Todo está listo: jamón español, tortilla y paella.

Elena: ¿Qué lleva la paella?

José: Esta paella tiene arroz, pollo y gambas.

Elena: Ay, tengo alergia a las gambas.

José: Vaya,no lo sabía.Lo siento. No pasa nada porque también tengo queso y vino español.

Elena: Genial. Voy a probar la tortilla. ¿Es la famosa tor5lla española?

José: Sí, claro. ¿Te gusta?

Elena: ¡Mmmmmh! Está muy rica. ¿Cuál es tu secreto?

José: El secreto está en cocinar con mucho amor.

José: Hi, Elena! Welcome to my Spanish dinner.

Elena: Thanks for invi5ng me. Shall I help you with anything?

José: There's no need to. Everything is ready: Spanish ham, omelede and paella.

Elena: What is in the paella?

José: This paella is made with rice, chicken and prawns.

Elena: Uh, I'm allergic to prawns.

José: Oh dear, I didn't know. I'm sorry. But don't worry, I've also got Spanish cheese and wine.

Elena: Fantastic. I'll try the omelede. Is this the famous Spanish tortilla?

José: Yes it is. Do you like it?

Elena: Mmmmmh! It's really delicious. What's your secret?

José: The secret lies in cooking with lots of love.

ENTREVISTA DE EMPLEO - JOB INTERVIEW

Example 1:

Entrevistador: Hola señor ¿Puede responderme unas preguntas, por favor? **Pablo:** Sí, por supuesto. **Entrevistador:** ¿Cómo se llama? **Pablo:** Me llamo Pablo. **Entrevistador:** Pablo. ¿Qué piensas acerca de las nuevas tecnologías? **Pablo:** Pienso que son estupendas y nos ayudan con las tareas más dieciles **Entrevistador: Gracias.**	**Interviewer:** Hello sir, can you answer a few questions for me, please? **Pablo:** Yes, of course. **Interviewer:** What is your name? **Pablo:** My name is Pablo. **Interviewer:** Pablo. What do you think about new technologies. **Pablo:** I think they are great and help us with the most difficult tasks. **Interviewer:** Thank you.

Example 2:

Secretaria: Señor Rodriguez puede entrar. El señor López le espera. **Luis:** Buenos días señor Rodriguéz. **Elías:** Buenos días. **Luis:** Por favor siéntese. ¿Ha traído su currículo? **Elías:** Sí, aqui está. **Luis:** Señor Rodriguez ¿Qué hace usted actualmente? **Elías:** Actualmente estoy en el paro.	**Secretary:** Mr. Rodriguez can enter. Mr. López awaits you. **Luis:** Good morning Mr. Rodriguez. **Elías:** Good morning. **Louis:** Please sit down. Have you brought your resume? **Elías:** Yes, here he is. **Luis:** Mr. Rodriguez, what are you currently doing? **Elías:** I am currently unemployed.

Luis: ¿Por qué dejo su úl5mo empleo?

Elías: Porque se terminó el contrato con la empresa en que yo trabajaba.

Luis: Sí ¿Por qué mo5vo usted quiere ser el nuevo asistente de mercadeo en nuestra empresa?

Elías: Es que me gusta mucho trabajar con publicidad y mercadeo.

Luis: ¿Qué sabe usted sabe acerca de nuestra empresa?

Elías: Esta empresa es la mayor empresa de mercadeo hoy en España y de reconocimiento mundial por sus optimas campañas desarrolladas.

Luis: ¿Está dispuesto usted a viajar con frecuencia?

Elías: Sí estoy, además soy una persona que tengo facilidad de adaptarme a lo nuevo.

Luis: ¿Cómo le gusta trabajar? ¿Prefiere trabajar sólo o en equipo?

Elías: Prefiero trabajar en equipo pero también puedo trabajar sólo sin problemas.

Luis: ¿Por qué prefiere trabajar en equipo?

Elías: Para poder desarrollar un servicio mejor.

Luis: Why did you leave your last job?

Elías: Because the contract with the company I worked for ended.

Luis: Yes, why do you want to be the new marketing assistant in our company?

Elías: I really like working with advertising and marketing.

Luis: What do you know about our company?

Elías: This company is the largest marketing company in Spain today and is world-renowned for its excellent campaigns.

Luis: Are you willing to travel frequently?

Elías: Yes, I am, I am also a person who easily adapts to new things.

Luis: How do you like to work? Would you rather work alone or in a group?

Elías: I prefer to work in a team but I can also work alone without problems.

Luis: Why do you prefer to work in a team?

Elías: To be able to develop a beder service.

Luis: ¿Cuáles son sus puntos fuertes y débiles?	**Luis:** What are your strengths and weaknesses?
Elías: Soy muy crea5vo, tengo facilidad en desarrollar proyectos que exigen gran capacidad de crea5vidad y concentración.	**Elías:** I am very creative, I am able to develop projects that require a great capacity for creativity and concentration.
Luis: ¿Y débiles?	**Luis:** And weak?
Elías: Soy algo nervioso a veces.	**Elías:** I am somewhat nervous at times.
Luis: ¿Cuáles son sus obje5vos a medio y a largo plazo?	**Luis:** What are your medium and long-term goals?

Vocabulario relacionado con empleo – Vocabulary related to getting a job

Candidate - Aspirante
Space available - Vacante
Career - Carrera
Salary - Salario
Comissions - Comisiones
Post / Role – Puesto
Employee - Empregado
Employer - Empregador

Estoy buscando un nuevo trabajo. - I'm looking for a new job.
Mi sueldo es muy bajo. - My salary is very low.
¿Qué puesto quiere ocupar? - What role do you like to occupy?

EXAMPLE DIALOGS

CHRISTMAS SHOPPING

Fernando: ¿Ya han comprado los regalos de navidad? **Sara:** Oscar no ha comprado nada y yo he comprado de todo. **Fernando:** ¿Qué has comprado? **Sara: Sara:** He comprado juguetes, videojuegos y pantalones de lona. **Fernando:** ¿Cuánto has gastado? **Sara:** He gastado más de 200 euros. **Fernando:** Has gastado bastante. **Sara:** Y tú ¿has comprado ya algo? **Fernando:** No, no he comprado nada. No he trabajado todo el año.	**Fernando:** Have you all already purchased the Christmas presents? **Sara:** Oscar has not bought anything and I have bought everything. **Fernando:** What have you bought? **Sara:** I have bought toys, video-games and canvas trousers. **Fernando:** How much have you spent? **Sara:** I have spent more than 200 euros. **Fernando:** You have spent a lot. **Sara:** And you, have you already bought something? **Fernando:** No, I didn't bought anything. I have not worked all year.

LIVING IN THE CITY

Rosa: ¡Buenos días Pedro! ¿Qué te pasa hoy? Parece que estás enfadado.
Pedro: Buenos días, no estoy enfadado, en realidad sólo estoy cansado. Todos los días lo mismo… ¡Qué aburrido!
Rosa: ¿Por qué no haces algo divertido? Hayque intentar animarse.
Pedro: Ya sabes cuantas horas trabajo… no tengo mucho tiempo ni energía para hacer lo que me gusta.
Rosa: ¿Y qué te gustaría hacer?
Pedro: Me gustaría pasar más 5empo en el campo, pero trabajo todos los días de 8.00 a 18.30 h. No sé… no me gusta vivir en la ciudad hay mucho ruido y mucho tráfico.
Rosa: Estoy totalmente de acuerdo contigo. Sólo me siento completamente tranquila y relajada cuando estoy cerca del mar. Echo de menos esa sensación…

Rosa: Good morning, Pedro! What's up? You look like you are angry.
Pedro: Good morning, I am not angry, I'm just really tired. Every day the same… How boring!

Rosa: Why don't you do something fun? We have to cheer up.
Pedro: You know how many hours I work… I do not have much time nor energy to do things I like.
Rosa: And what do you like to do?
Pedro: I would spend more time in the field, but I work every day from 8 a.m. to 6 p.m. . I don't know… I don't like living in the city, it's noisy and heavy traffic.
Rosa: I totally agree with you. I just feel completely calm and relaxed when I'm near the sea. I miss that feeling…

THE CHAIR

Julia: Necesito una silla.	**Julia:** I need a chair.
Daniel: ¿Para qué quieres una silla?	**Daniel:** Why do you want a chair?
Julia: Para la terraza.	**Julia:** For the terrace.
Daniel: ¿Qué 5po de silla quieres?	**Daniel:** What type of chair do you want?
Julia: Una mecedora.	**Julia:** A rocking-chair.
Daniel: ¿Para qué quieres una mecedora?	**Daniel:** Why do you want a rocking-chair?
Julia: Para descansar. ¡Mira esta qué linda!	**Julia:** To relax. Look at this, how beautiful!
Daniel: ¿Puedo sentarme?	**Daniel:** May I sit down?
Julia: ¿Qué te parece?	**Julia:** What do think?
Daniel: Muy cómoda.	**Daniel:** Very comfortable.
Julia: ¿Me la compras?	**Julia:** Will you buy it for me?
Daniel: Mmm… ¡claro!	**Daniel: Mmm… certainly!**

VACACIONES - VACATIONS

El campamento - **Camping**
La playa - **Beach**
El crucero - **Cruise**
El campo - **Countryside**

¿Cuándo vas a coger vacaciones? - **When are you going on vacaction?**

¿Qué vas a hacer en tus vacaciones? - **What are you going to do on your vacations?**

¿Cuánto cuesta el pasaje? - **How much is the pocket?**

No se pare en el bote cuando este se esté moviendo. - **Don't stand up in the boat while it is moving around.**

Asegurate de tomar el bus en el horario que funciona. - **Be sure to take the bus in the schedule it works.**

- Documentos para viajar – **travel documentation**
- El seguro de viaje – **travel insurance**
- Una prueba negativa de COVID-19 – **COVID-19 negative test**
- Los registros de salud – **health records**
- El puerto – **port**
- La zona de embarque – **boarding area**
- El recuerdo - **the souvenir**
- El regalo - **the present, the gift**

- El billete de ida y vuelta - **the round-trip ticket**
- Los boletos de avión - **airplane tickets**
- La maleta - **the suitcase, the bag**
- El turista - **the tourist, the vacationer**
- El paisaje - **the landscape**
- Las vistas - **the view**
- El mar - **the sea**
- La agencia de viajes - **the travel agency**
- La queja, la reclamación - **the complaint**
- La sombrilla - **the shade, the umbrella**
- La escala - **the stopover**
- El auxiliar de vuelo - **the flight attendant**
- La atracción turística - **the tourist attraction**
- El casco antiguo - **the old town, the historical center - the suitcase, the bag**

Some verbs that you are going to need:
- Viajar, ir de viaje, hacer un viaje - **to travel, to go on a trip**
- Estar de vacaciones - **to be on vacation**
- Hacer fotos - **to take pictures**
- Hacer una excursión- **to go for a ramble**
- Hacer una reserva, reservar - **to make a reservation, to book**
- Hacer las maletas - **to pack, to pack your luggage**
- Visitar - **to visit, to tour, to see, to go**
- Tomar un taxi - **to take a taxi**
- Quedarse - **to stay (like at a hotel)**
- Descansar - **to rest**
- Alquilar - **to rent**
- Divertirse, disfrutar, pasárselo bien - **to have fun, to have a blast, to enjoy oneself**
- Ver los lugares de interés - **to visit places of interest**
- Dar un paseo - **to go for a walk**
- Ir a pie - **to go on foot**

AUTHOR BIO

Adriana Muñoz loves languages.

As a Spanish-American, she served as a linguist for six years in the United States Navy before continuing her language proficiencies by teaching others who want to learn them as a second language or improve on their native tongue.

She's fluent in Spanish, Portuguese, French, English, and Arabic.

Adrian grew up in Spain and now resides in America with her family, and publishes language learning books to help those traveling or just wanting to learn another language.

Copyright © 2022 Adriana Muñoz

All rights reserved. No part of this guide may be
reproduced in any form without permission in writing from
the publisher except in the case of brief quotations
embodied in critical articles or reviews.

Made in United States
Orlando, FL
10 February 2023

29820098R00043